The Conflict Resolution Library

Dealing with Weapons at School and at Home

• Lorelei Apel •

The Rosen Publishing Group's
PowerKids Press
New York

Published in 1996 by The Rosen Publishing Group, Inc.
29 East 21st Street, New York, NY 10010

Copyright © 1996 by The Rosen Publishing Group, Inc.

Photo credits: Cover photo by Maria Moreno; p. 4 © Christopher Morris/International Stock; p. 15 © Jeff Greenberg/International Stock; p. 16 © Tom McKitterick/Impact Visuals; all other photos by Maria Moreno.

First Edition

Layout and design: Erin McKenna

Apel, Lorelei.
    Dealing with weapons at school and at home / Lorelei Apel.
        p.   cm.
    Includes index.
    Summary: Points out the danger of having weapons at school and at home and offers tips on how to avoid getting hurt or hurting others.
    ISBN 0-8239-2327-4
    1. Gun control—United States—Juvenile literature. 2. Firearms ownership—United States—Juvenile literature. 3. School violence—United States—Prevention—Juvenile literature. 4. Firearms—United States—Safety measures—Juvenile literature. 5. Weapons—United States—Safety measures—Juvenile literature. [1. Gun control. 2. Firearms ownership. 3. School violence. 4. Violence. 5. Firearms—Safety measures. 6. Weapons—Safety measures. 7. Safety.] I. Title. II. Series.
    HV7436.A58 1996
    363.3'3'0973—dc20   95-50792
                                                                  CIP
                                                                  AC

Manufactured in the United States of America

Contents

What Is a Weapon?

A **weapon** (WEP-un) is something used to hurt people. It can be a gun, a knife, or even a baseball bat if it's used in the wrong way.

Weapons can be useful. Police officers carry weapons to protect people. Your parents might have a weapon to protect you and your family.

Weapons can also be **dangerous** (DANE-jer-us). Criminals and gangs use weapons to hurt people. Kids can get hurt with weapons.

◄ A police officer carries a gun and a nightstick to protect himself and other people.

Eddie and Jeff

One day Eddie invited his best friend Jeff over to show him his dad's new gun. Eddie took the gun out of the closet and began to make shooting noises like the ones he made when he played with his toy gun. Suddenly there was a loud "Bang!" Eddie and Jeff stared at a new hole in the wall. Eddie didn't realize that the gun was loaded. He could have hurt himself or his best friend.

You could hurt yourself or someone else by playing with a weapon. ▶

They Really Hurt!

We see weapons all the time. Actors use them on television. Many cartoon characters use weapons. Toy stores sell all kinds of toy guns, knives, and swords. Because we see weapons all the time, many people don't realize how dangerous they are. It is easy to forget that they can hurt or even kill people. In fact, between two and three thousand kids are shot and killed every year in the United States.

◀ We are so used to seeing toy weapons that we may not realize that real weapons can hurt us.

Weapons at Home

Having a weapon in your home can be dangerous. Your mom's gun might look like a toy, but it's not. You may want to play with your dad's hunting knife, but it can hurt you.

It is important *never* to touch a weapon that your parent might have at home, or that you might see in a friend's house. A gun or a knife or another type of weapon can hurt you.

It is important never to touch a weapon no matter where you see it. ▶

Weapons at School

Sometimes kids take weapons to school. Some kids think that having a weapon makes them powerful. Some kids carry a weapon to protect themselves from gangs or bullies. Other kids think they can use weapons to solve problems with other students or teachers.

None of these kids realize that carrying a weapon doesn't solve problems. It only makes problems worse.

◀ You may have seen someone carrying a weapon at school.

13

Ben's Choice

Ben was often in trouble. One day he was running through the hallways. This was against the rules. Mrs. Davis, his teacher, asked Ben to stop running. He said no. Mrs. Davis told Ben to go to the principal's office. While he was waiting for the principal, Ben thought about the knife he had in his backpack. He wanted to hurt Mrs. Davis, but he knew that was wrong. Ben decided to throw the knife away.

Weapons cause problems. They don't solve them. ▶

Taking Action in School

Many kids are hurt by weapons each year. People want to stop this from happening. Some schools use **metal detectors** (MET-al dee-TEK-tors) to see if any students are carrying weapons. Then the weapons are taken away. This makes school a safer place to learn.

Some schools have **security guards** (se-KYUR-i-tee GARDS). Their job is to protect students and teachers from weapons and violence.

Some junior high and high schools use metal detectors and security guards to keep weapons out of their schools.

Talking It Out

Some kids use weapons because they don't know how to talk about their problems. Talking to a friend or an adult about how you feel makes you feel better. It is more grown-up to talk than to hurt someone with a weapon. If you tell someone how you are feeling, that person can help you solve the problem or feel better.

Talking to someone about how you feel can make you feel better. ▶

What You Can Do at Home

If your parents have a weapon at home, here are some things you can do to help make sure that you, your brothers and sisters, and your friends don't get hurt by it.

- Ask your parent to keep the weapon locked up in a safe place out of your reach and the reach of younger brothers or sisters.
- Don't ever play with guns, knives, or other weapons.
- Teach your brothers and sisters to stay away from weapons.

◀ You put your toy weapons in a safe place. Ask your parents to put their real weapons in a safe place.

What You Can Do at School

You can help keep your school safe too.
- Never carry a weapon to school.
- If you know someone at school has a weapon, tell a teacher. But tell them **secretly** (SEE-kret-lee) so that other kids don't know who reported it.
- If someone threatens you with a weapon, give him what he wants. Don't fight back.
- Never try to take a weapon away from someone. You could get hurt.

Glossary

dangerous (DANE-jer-us) Able to cause harm to
   someone.
metal detector (MET-al dee-TEK-tor) Machine
   used to tell if someone is carrying a metal
   weapon.
secretly (SEE-kret-lee) Doing something so that
   nobody knows about it.
security guard (se-KYUR-i-tee GARD) Person
   hired to keep a place safe.
weapon (WEP-un) Something that can hurt
   someone.

23

Index